Table of Contents

Introduction: ---3
Chapter 1: The Journey Begins --5
Chapter 2: Defining Your Vision -------------------------------------8
Chapter 3: Cultivating Self-Awareness -----------------------------12
Chapter 4: Building Emotional Intelligence ------------------------16
Chapter 5: Mastering Communication Skills -----------------------19
Chapter 6: Developing a Leadership Style ------------------------22
Chapter 7: Building a High-Performing Team --------------------26
Chapter 8: Leading with Integrity ------------------------------------30
Chapter 9: Managing Change and Uncertainty ------------------34
Chapter 10: Cultivating Innovation and Creativity ---------------38
Chapter 11: Strategic Thinking and Decision-Making -----------42
Chapter 12: Leading Through Crisis --------------------------------46
Chapter 13: Inspiring and Motivating Others ----------------------50
Chapter 14: Mentoring and Developing Others -------------------53
Chapter 15: Influencing and Negotiating ---------------------------55
Chapter 16: Managing Time and Priorities -------------------------59
Chapter 17: Leading with Resilience ---------------------------------63
Chapter 18: Embracing Diversity and Inclusion -------------------67
Chapter 19: Leading in a Global Context ---------------------------70
Chapter 20: Balancing Work and Life --------------------------------74
Chapter 21: Nurturing Continuous Learning------------------------77

Chapter 22: Leading with Authenticity ------------------------------82

Chapter 23: Managing Stakeholder Relationships ---------------84

Chapter 24: Leveraging Technology for Leadership --------------89

Chapter 25: Reflecting and Evolving as a Leader------------------93

Chapter 26: Leading with Empathy and Compassion ------------97

Chapter 27: Overcoming Leadership Challenges ----------------101

Chapter 28: Leaving a Leadership Legacy -------------------------105

Chapter 29: Leading with Purpose and Passion------------------108

Chapter 30: The Journey Continues ---------------------------------111

Introduction:

"Rise to Lead: Unleashing Your Potential" is an empowering and transformative book that serves as a guide for individuals seeking to tap into their true leadership potential. Drawing upon a wealth of wisdom, personal anecdotes, and practical strategies, this book takes readers on a transformative journey towards self-discovery and personal growth.

The book begins by challenging traditional notions of leadership and redefines it as a universal quality that exists within everyone, rather than being limited to a select few. It emphasizes the idea that leadership is not restricted to formal positions of authority but can be expressed in various domains of life, including personal relationships, career choices, and community engagement.

Through insightful storytelling and thought-provoking exercises, "Rise to Lead" encourages readers to explore their unique strengths, passions, and values. It offers a step-by-step roadmap to help individuals identify their core purpose, unleash their innate talents, and overcome self-imposed limitations. The book emphasizes the importance of self-awareness, self-mastery, and fostering meaningful connections with others to lead authentically and effectively.

As readers progress through the book, they encounter practical tools and strategies to develop essential leadership skills such as effective communication, decision-making, problem-solving, and resilience. It delves into the power of emotional intelligence, empathy, and adaptability in building strong relationships and creating positive change.

Moreover, "Rise to Lead" addresses the challenges and obstacles that individuals may encounter on their leadership journey, providing valuable insights and guidance to navigate through setbacks, embrace failure as a learning opportunity, and maintain a growth mindset.

Whether you're a student, professional, entrepreneur, or anyone seeking to make a meaningful impact, "Rise to Lead" serves as a trusted companion, offering practical advice and inspiration to unlock your full leadership potential. By the end of the book, readers will have gained a deep understanding of their unique leadership style and the confidence to embrace opportunities, make a difference, and inspire others to do the same.

"Rise to Lead: Unleashing Your Potential" is a compelling and transformative read that empowers individuals to become authentic and influential leaders, both in their personal and professional lives. It inspires readers to rise above their limitations, embrace their true potential, and create a positive impact in their spheres of influence.

Chapter 1: The Journey Begins

Introduction to the book and its purpose

Welcome to the first chapter of our book, where we embark on a transformative journey of self-discovery and leadership development. This book is designed to empower and inspire you to unlock your true potential as a leader. Whether you are already in a leadership position or aspire to become one, this book will provide valuable insights, practical tips, and thought-provoking exercises to help you grow and excel.

In this chapter, we lay the foundation for our exploration by delving into the concept of leadership and understanding its significance in today's world. We will also delve into the importance of self-awareness and recognizing the potential that lies within you. Remember, leadership is not limited to a title or a position; it is a mindset and a set of skills that can be cultivated by anyone willing to put in the effort.

Exploring the concept of leadership

Leadership is a multifaceted concept that goes beyond simply being in charge or giving orders. It is about inspiring and influencing others to achieve a common goal, while fostering an environment of collaboration, growth, and positive change. A true leader possesses qualities such as vision, integrity, empathy, resilience, and the ability to communicate effectively.

In this chapter, we will delve deeper into these qualities and explore how they contribute to effective leadership. We will also discuss different leadership styles and approaches, as well as the importance of adapting your style to suit different situations and individuals. Remember, leadership is not a one-size-fits-all concept. It is about understanding yourself, your team, and the context in which you operate.

Identifying the potential within yourself

Each and every one of us has untapped potential waiting to be discovered and nurtured. In this section, we will guide you through a process of self-reflection and introspection to help you identify your unique strengths, values, and passions. Understanding these aspects of yourself will not only enhance your self-awareness but also enable you to lead authentically.

We will also explore the concept of mindset and its impact on your leadership journey. Cultivating a growth mindset, which embraces challenges, learns from failures, and seeks continuous improvement, is crucial for personal and professional development. By developing a positive and resilient mindset, you will be better equipped to face the inevitable obstacles and setbacks that come with leadership.

Throughout this chapter, we encourage you to engage in reflective exercises and journaling prompts to deepen your understanding of yourself and your leadership potential. By the end of this chapter, you will have laid the groundwork for your leadership journey, armed with newfound insights and a greater sense of purpose.

So, let's begin this transformative adventure together as we unravel the mysteries of leadership and embark on a path of personal and professional growth. Get ready to discover the leader within you!

Chapter 2: Defining Your Vision

Section 1: Understanding the Power of Vision in Leadership

Vision plays a crucial role in effective leadership. It provides a clear direction and purpose, inspiring and guiding both leaders and their teams towards a common goal. A strong vision helps to create a sense of unity, motivates individuals to go above and beyond, and enables them to overcome challenges along the way. By understanding the power of vision, leaders can harness its potential to drive meaningful change and achieve extraordinary results.

Section 2: Techniques for Clarifying and Articulating Your Vision

2.1 Reflection and Self-Assessment: Start by reflecting on your values, strengths, and passions. Consider what you want to accomplish and how you can make a positive impact. Conduct a self-assessment to identify your core beliefs and areas where you excel. This self-reflection will help you align your vision with your authentic self.

2.2 Engage in Strategic Thinking: Think long-term and consider the broader implications of your vision. Analyze trends, anticipate future challenges, and envision how your goals align with the needs of your organization, community, or industry. Engaging in strategic thinking allows you to develop a vision that is both forward-looking and realistic.

2.3 Seek Inspiration and Input: Look for inspiration from various sources, including successful leaders, industry trends, and innovative ideas. Gather input from key stakeholders, colleagues, and team members to gain diverse perspectives. This collaborative approach ensures that your vision incorporates a wide range of insights, making it more comprehensive and relevant.

2.4 Define Core Values: Clearly define the core values that will underpin your vision. These values should guide your decision-making and serve as a compass for your actions. When your vision is aligned with your core values, it creates a strong foundation for sustainable and ethical leadership.

2.5 Craft a Compelling Narrative: Transform your vision into a compelling story that captures the imagination of others. Use vivid language, imagery, and metaphors to communicate your vision in a way that resonates emotionally. A well-crafted narrative helps people connect with your vision on a deeper level and fosters a shared understanding.

Section 3: Setting Meaningful Goals to Align with Your Vision

3.1 Start with the End in Mind: Begin by envisioning the desired outcome that reflects your vision. What does success look like? Visualize the ultimate goal and work backward to identify the steps needed to achieve it. This approach ensures that your goals are aligned with your broader vision.

3.2 SMART Goal Setting: Set Specific, Measurable, Achievable, Relevant, and Time-bound (SMART) goals that are directly linked to your vision. Clearly define each goal, quantify its progress, ensure its feasibility, align it with your vision's purpose, and set a realistic timeline for completion. SMART goals help you stay focused and track progress effectively.

3.3 Break Down Goals into Milestones: Divide your long-term goals into smaller milestones or objectives. Breaking down goals into manageable chunks provides a sense of accomplishment as each milestone is achieved, maintaining motivation and momentum throughout the journey.

3.4 Foster Accountability and Collaboration: Share your goals and milestones with your team or trusted individuals. Encourage their active participation, feedback, and suggestions. This fosters a sense of accountability, collective ownership, and promotes collaboration, ultimately increasing the likelihood of achieving the shared vision.

3.5 Monitor and Adjust: Continuously monitor your progress towards your goals and adjust your strategies as necessary. Regularly review and assess the alignment between your goals and vision. Adaptation and flexibility are essential to navigate unforeseen challenges and seize new opportunities along the way.

By applying these techniques, leaders can define a compelling vision, articulate it effectively, and set meaningful goals that align with that vision. This chapter serves as a foundation for the subsequent chapters, where we will delve deeper into executing your vision, inspiring others, and leading through change.

Chapter 3: Cultivating Self-Awareness

Introduction:
Self-awareness is a fundamental trait for effective leadership. It involves having a deep understanding of one's own emotions, strengths, weaknesses, values, and impact on others. In this chapter, we will explore the importance of self-awareness in leadership, how to assess your strengths and weaknesses, and how to develop a growth mindset to enhance your self-awareness.

Section 1: The Importance of Self-Awareness in Leadership

Effective leaders possess a high level of self-awareness, as it allows them to understand their own behavior, motivations, and reactions. Self-awareness enables leaders to make conscious decisions, regulate their emotions, and respond to challenges with greater empathy and understanding. It also enhances their ability to build and maintain meaningful relationships with their team members and stakeholders.

Subsection 1.1: Enhanced Decision-Making

Self-aware leaders are better equipped to make sound decisions because they understand their own biases, values, and triggers. They can evaluate situations objectively and consider multiple perspectives before arriving at a well-informed conclusion. By being aware of their own strengths and weaknesses, leaders can delegate tasks effectively and seek assistance in areas where they lack expertise.

Subsection 1.2: Improved Emotional Intelligence

Self-awareness is closely linked to emotional intelligence, which is crucial for effective leadership. Leaders who are self-aware can recognize and manage their emotions, as well as understand how their emotions impact others. This enables them to create a positive work environment, handle conflicts constructively, and motivate their team members.

Section 2: Assessing Your Strengths and Weaknesses

To cultivate self-awareness, leaders must assess their strengths and weaknesses objectively. This assessment provides a clear understanding of areas where they excel and areas that require improvement.

Subsection 2.1: Seeking Feedback

Leaders should actively seek feedback from their peers, team members, and superiors. Constructive feedback offers valuable insights into blind spots and areas for development. Creating a safe and open feedback culture encourages honest communication, fosters personal growth, and strengthens leadership effectiveness.

Subsection 2.2: Reflective Practices

Engaging in reflective practices, such as journaling, self-assessment exercises, and introspection, allows leaders to gain deeper insights into their thoughts, feelings, and actions. Reflective practices promote self-discovery, helping leaders uncover patterns of behavior and identify areas where they can grow and improve.

Section 3: Developing a Growth Mindset
A growth mindset is the belief that one's abilities and intelligence can be developed through effort, practice, and learning. Cultivating a growth mindset is essential for self-awareness and continuous personal development.

Subsection 3.1: Embracing Challenges
Leaders with a growth mindset view challenges as opportunities for learning and growth. They embrace new experiences, seek out challenging tasks, and approach setbacks as stepping stones to future success. By reframing failure as a learning experience, leaders can maintain a positive attitude and persevere in the face of obstacles.

Subsection 3.2: Cultivating Curiosity and Learning
Leaders with a growth mindset are curious and open to new ideas. They actively seek knowledge, engage in lifelong learning, and encourage a culture of continuous improvement within their teams. By staying intellectually curious and adapting to changing circumstances, leaders can remain agile and better navigate complex and dynamic environments.

Conclusion:
Self-awareness is a foundational skill for effective leadership. By understanding their strengths and weaknesses and cultivating a growth mindset, leaders can enhance their self-awareness and unlock their full potential. Through continuous self-reflection and a commitment to personal development, leaders can build stronger relationships, make better decisions, and inspire their teams to achieve remarkable outcomes.

Chapter 4: Building Emotional Intelligence

Introduction:
In this chapter, we will explore the concept of emotional intelligence and its significance in effective leadership. Emotional intelligence refers to the ability to recognize, understand, and manage one's own emotions, as well as the emotions of others. It plays a crucial role in leadership, as leaders who possess high emotional intelligence can inspire, motivate, and build strong relationships with their team members. We will delve into the key components of emotional intelligence, namely self-regulation, empathy, and interpersonal relationships, and discuss strategies for developing and strengthening these skills.

Section 1: Understanding Emotional Intelligence and Its Impact on Leadership
1.1 Defining Emotional Intelligence: We will provide a clear definition of emotional intelligence, emphasizing its importance in leadership roles.
1.2 Components of Emotional Intelligence: We will explore the four main components of emotional intelligence: self-awareness, self-regulation, empathy, and social skills. We will explain how each component contributes to effective leadership.
1.3 The Impact of Emotional Intelligence on Leadership: We will discuss the ways in which emotional intelligence positively influences leadership, including improved communication, decision-making, and team dynamics.

Section 2: Developing Self-Regulation and Empathy

2.1 Self-Regulation: We will delve into the concept of self-regulation, which involves managing one's own emotions, impulses, and reactions. We will discuss strategies for enhancing self-regulation, such as practicing self-reflection, mindfulness techniques, and stress management.

2.2 Empathy: We will explore the importance of empathy in leadership and its ability to foster stronger connections with team members. We will provide practical techniques for developing empathy, including active listening, perspective-taking, and showing genuine concern for others.

Section 3: Strengthening Interpersonal Relationships

3.1 Building Trust: We will emphasize the role of trust in interpersonal relationships and leadership effectiveness. We will discuss strategies for building trust, such as consistent communication, transparency, and delivering on commitments.

3.2 Effective Communication: We will highlight the significance of effective communication in building strong relationships. We will provide tips for improving communication skills, including active listening, clarity, and nonverbal cues.

3.3 Conflict Resolution: We will address the inevitability of conflicts in interpersonal relationships and present strategies for resolving them constructively. We will emphasize the importance of maintaining emotional intelligence during conflict situations and seeking win-win outcomes.

Conclusion:

In this chapter, we have explored the concept of emotional intelligence and its impact on leadership. We have discussed the importance of self-regulation, empathy, and strong interpersonal relationships for effective leadership. By developing these aspects of emotional intelligence, leaders can foster a positive work environment, inspire their teams, and achieve collective goals. We have provided practical strategies and techniques for building emotional intelligence, and we encourage readers to incorporate these skills into their leadership practices.

Chapter 5: Mastering Communication Skills

Effective communication is a crucial tool for effective leadership. In this chapter, we will explore the importance of communication skills in leadership and how they can be developed and mastered. We will also delve into two key aspects of communication: active listening and impactful speaking. Additionally, we will discuss strategies for navigating difficult conversations successfully.

Section 1: Effective Communication as a Leadership Tool
Effective communication lies at the heart of successful leadership. Leaders who can convey their vision, inspire their team, and foster collaboration are more likely to achieve their goals. In this section, we will explore the following topics:

1.1 The Role of Communication in Leadership
   - The impact of effective communication on team productivity and morale
   - Building trust and credibility through clear and consistent communication
   - Aligning goals and expectations through effective communication

1.2 Developing Your Communication Style as a Leader
   - Understanding your own communication strengths and weaknesses
   - Adapting your style to different audiences and situations

- Building rapport and establishing connections through communication

Section 2: Listening Actively and Speaking with Impact
Communication is a two-way process that involves both listening and speaking. In this section, we will focus on honing these skills to become a more effective communicator:

2.1 Active Listening
   - The importance of active listening in understanding others
   - Techniques for active listening, such as paraphrasing and asking clarifying questions
   - Nonverbal cues and body language in active listening

2.2 Speaking with Impact
   - Crafting clear and concise messages that resonate with your audience
   - Using storytelling and anecdotes to engage and inspire others
   - Developing confident and persuasive speaking skills

Section 3: Navigating Difficult Conversations
Leaders often encounter difficult conversations, such as giving constructive feedback, addressing conflicts, or managing challenging situations. In this section, we will explore strategies to navigate such conversations effectively:

3.1 Preparing for Difficult Conversations

- Setting goals and planning the conversation in advance
- Managing emotions and maintaining a calm and professional demeanor
- Anticipating potential challenges and preparing responses

3.2 Effective Communication Techniques in Difficult Conversations

- Active listening and empathetic communication to understand others' perspectives
- Assertiveness and clarity in expressing your own thoughts and concerns
- Managing conflicts and finding common ground for resolution

Conclusion:
Mastering communication skills is a fundamental aspect of effective leadership. By developing strong communication skills, leaders can inspire their teams, foster collaboration, and navigate difficult conversations with confidence. In the next chapter, we will explore the role of emotional intelligence in leadership and how it complements effective communication.

Chapter 6: Developing a Leadership Style

Introduction:
In this chapter, we will delve into the topic of leadership styles and how they impact your effectiveness as a leader. We will explore various leadership styles, help you identify your personal style, and discuss the importance of adapting your style to different situations and individuals. Developing a well-rounded leadership style is crucial for achieving success and influencing those around you.

Section 1: Exploring Different Leadership Styles
1.1 Autocratic Leadership:
   - Definition and characteristics of autocratic leadership
   - Advantages and disadvantages of autocratic leadership
   - Examples of situations where autocratic leadership is appropriate

1.2 Democratic Leadership:
   - Definition and characteristics of democratic leadership
   - Advantages and disadvantages of democratic leadership
   - Examples of situations where democratic leadership is appropriate

1.3 Laissez-Faire Leadership:
   - Definition and characteristics of laissez-faire leadership
   - Advantages and disadvantages of laissez-faire leadership
   - Examples of situations where laissez-faire leadership is appropriate

1.4 Transformational Leadership:
  - Definition and characteristics of transformational leadership
  - Advantages and disadvantages of transformational leadership
  - Examples of situations where transformational leadership is appropriate

1.5 Transactional Leadership:
  - Definition and characteristics of transactional leadership
  - Advantages and disadvantages of transactional leadership
  - Examples of situations where transactional leadership is appropriate

Section 2: Identifying Your Personal Leadership Style
2.1 Self-Assessment:
  - Reflecting on your strengths, weaknesses, values, and beliefs
  - Identifying your natural tendencies in leadership situations

2.2 Leadership Style Models:
  - Introduction to popular leadership style models (e.g., Hersey-Blanchard, Blake-Mouton)
  - Assessing your leadership style using these models
  - Understanding the implications of your leadership style on your team

2.3 Feedback and Reflection:
   - Seeking feedback from colleagues, subordinates, and mentors
   - Reflecting on your past leadership experiences
   - Identifying patterns and areas for improvement

Section 3: Adapting Your Style to Different Situations and Individuals

3.1 Situational Leadership:
   - Understanding the importance of adapting your leadership style to different situations
   - Assessing the competence and commitment of your team members
   - Matching leadership style to the developmental level of individuals or teams

3.2 Emotional Intelligence:
   - Developing emotional intelligence as a leader
   - Recognizing and adapting to the emotions and needs of others
   - Using empathy and self-awareness to tailor your leadership approach

3.3 Flexibility and Agility:
   - Being open to change and adjusting your leadership style as needed
   - Recognizing the diverse needs and preferences of individuals
   - Balancing consistency with adaptability

Conclusion:

Developing an effective leadership style is a continuous journey that requires self-awareness, flexibility, and a willingness to grow. By exploring different leadership styles, identifying your personal style, and adapting to different situations and individuals, you can become a more versatile and influential leader. Remember that leadership is not a one-size-fits-all approach, and the key is to find a style that aligns with your values and the needs of your team.

Chapter 7: Building a High-Performing Team

Introduction:
Building a high-performing team is crucial for achieving success in any organization. In this chapter, we will explore key aspects of creating a positive team culture, selecting and developing team members, and fostering collaboration and synergy within the team. By focusing on these areas, leaders can cultivate an environment that promotes teamwork, creativity, and productivity.

Section 1: Creating a Positive Team Culture
A positive team culture is the foundation for a high-performing team. It sets the tone for how team members interact, communicate, and work together. Here are some strategies for creating a positive team culture:

1. Establish a shared purpose: Clearly define the team's mission, vision, and goals. Ensure that every team member understands and aligns with these objectives. A shared purpose provides a sense of direction and fosters a collective sense of ownership.

2. Encourage open communication: Create an environment where team members feel comfortable expressing their ideas, concerns, and opinions. Foster open and honest communication channels, both formal and informal, to facilitate collaboration and feedback.

3. Promote mutual respect and trust: Encourage team members to value each other's contributions and perspectives. Establish trust by promoting transparency, fairness, and accountability. Encourage constructive feedback and discourage negative behaviors such as gossip or blame.

4. Recognize and celebrate achievements: Acknowledge individual and team accomplishments regularly. Celebrate milestones and successes, which boosts morale, motivation, and a sense of belonging within the team.

Section 2: Selecting and Developing Team Members
Selecting the right team members is crucial for building a high-performing team. Here are some considerations when selecting and developing team members:

1. Define the required skills and competencies: Clearly define the skills, knowledge, and experience needed for each role within the team. This will help you identify individuals who possess the right qualifications and potential for growth.

2. Assess cultural fit: Consider the values, attitudes, and behaviors that align with the team's culture. Look for individuals who demonstrate a willingness to collaborate, adaptability, and a positive mindset.

3. Provide training and development opportunities: Invest in the professional development of team members. Offer training programs, workshops, or mentorship opportunities

to enhance their skills and knowledge. This not only improves individual performance but also contributes to the overall team's growth.

4. Foster a learning environment: Encourage a culture of continuous learning and improvement. Support team members in acquiring new skills, sharing knowledge, and experimenting with new ideas. Foster a growth mindset that embraces challenges and sees failures as opportunities for growth.

Section 3: Fostering Collaboration and Synergy
Effective collaboration and synergy are essential for achieving high performance. Here's how you can foster collaboration within your team:

1. Encourage teamwork: Emphasize the importance of collaboration and teamwork. Foster a sense of shared responsibility, where team members understand that their collective success is intertwined.

2. Establish clear roles and responsibilities: Define each team member's roles, responsibilities, and areas of expertise. This clarity minimizes conflicts and ensures that everyone understands their contributions to the team's objectives.

3. Promote cross-functional collaboration: Encourage collaboration across different departments or functional areas. Facilitate communication channels and

opportunities for teams to work together, share ideas, and leverage diverse perspectives.

4. Foster a supportive environment: Create a safe and supportive environment where team members feel comfortable taking risks, sharing ideas, and challenging the status quo. Encourage constructive feedback and provide resources or support to overcome obstacles.

Conclusion:
Building a high-performing team requires a deliberate focus on creating a positive team culture, selecting and developing team members, and fostering collaboration and synergy. By investing time and effort in these areas, leaders can create an environment that nurtures teamwork, empower individuals, and drives exceptional performance.

Chapter 8: Leading with Integrity

Introduction:
In the realm of leadership, ethics and integrity play a crucial role in defining the character and effectiveness of a leader. Leaders who prioritize ethical behavior and demonstrate integrity are more likely to inspire trust, build credibility, and foster a positive organizational culture. This chapter explores the significance of ethics and integrity in leadership, the process of making ethical decisions, and the methods for building trust and credibility.

1. The Role of Ethics and Integrity in Leadership:
a. Defining ethics and integrity: Ethics refers to the moral principles and values that guide behavior, while integrity involves consistency between one's actions, values, and beliefs. Both ethics and integrity are essential for leaders to establish a foundation of trust and inspire others to follow.

b. Setting the ethical tone: Leaders must set an example by embodying ethical behavior in their actions, decisions, and interactions. They should promote a culture of ethical conduct throughout the organization, emphasizing transparency, fairness, and accountability.

c. Influence on organizational culture: Leaders' ethical behavior significantly influences the culture of an organization. By prioritizing integrity and ethical decision-making, leaders create an environment that fosters trust, respect, and collaboration among team members.

2. Making Ethical Decisions:
a. Understanding ethical dilemmas: Leaders often encounter complex situations where they must navigate ethical dilemmas. These dilemmas involve conflicting values, interests, and potential consequences. It is essential for leaders to recognize and address these challenges effectively.

b. Ethical decision-making frameworks: Several frameworks can guide leaders in making ethical decisions, such as:
   i. Utilitarianism: Focusing on the greatest good for the greatest number of people.
   ii. Deontology: Emphasizing adherence to moral principles and duties.
   iii. Virtue ethics: Considering personal virtues and character traits.

c. Considering multiple perspectives: Leaders should actively seek diverse viewpoints and perspectives when confronted with ethical dilemmas. This inclusive approach helps to identify potential biases and make more well-rounded decisions.

d. Balancing short-term and long-term considerations: Ethical decision-making involves evaluating immediate outcomes as well as long-term consequences. Leaders should consider the potential impact of their decisions on stakeholders, the organization, and society as a whole.

3. Building Trust and Credibility:

a. Communication and transparency: Open and honest communication is vital for building trust. Leaders should provide clear expectations, share relevant information, and be transparent about their decisions and actions.

b. Consistency between words and actions: Leaders must demonstrate consistency between their stated values, commitments, and actual behavior. Inconsistencies erode trust and credibility.

c. Accountability and responsibility: Taking ownership of mistakes and holding oneself accountable for actions builds credibility. Leaders should foster a culture where individuals feel comfortable admitting and learning from their errors.

d. Empathy and respect: Leaders should demonstrate empathy and respect for their team members, valuing their opinions, and treating them fairly. This fosters trust, collaboration, and a positive work environment.

e. Encouraging ethical behavior: Leaders can promote ethical behavior by recognizing and rewarding individuals who exemplify integrity and ethics in their work. This reinforces the importance of ethical conduct throughout the organization.

Conclusion:
Leading with integrity is a fundamental aspect of effective leadership. By prioritizing ethics, making ethical decisions, and building trust and credibility, leaders can create a culture that empowers individuals, fosters collaboration, and drives organizational success. Ethical leaders serve as role models, inspiring others to embrace integrity and contribute to a positive and ethical work environment.

Chapter 9: Managing Change and Uncertainty

Introduction:
In today's dynamic and fast-paced business environment, change and uncertainty have become constant companions for leaders. The ability to navigate change, overcome resistance, and build resilience is crucial for effective leadership. In this chapter, we will explore strategies and techniques to help leaders manage change and uncertainty successfully.

Section 1: Navigating Change as a Leader
Change is often accompanied by challenges and complexities, but effective leaders can navigate through it by following these key strategies:

1. Embrace change: Recognize that change is inevitable and essential for growth and progress. Embracing change sets the tone for your team and encourages them to adopt a positive mindset.

2. Communicate openly: Provide clear and consistent communication to your team about the reasons for change, its benefits, and potential challenges. Transparency builds trust and helps alleviate anxiety or resistance.

3. Set a clear vision: Develop a compelling vision for the future and communicate it effectively. A well-defined vision provides direction and purpose, helping your team stay focused during times of change.

4. Lead by example: Demonstrate your commitment to change by embodying the behaviors and attitudes you expect from your team. Model adaptability, flexibility, and a willingness to learn.

5. Empower your team: Involve your team members in the change process. Encourage their input, listen to their concerns, and provide opportunities for them to contribute ideas and solutions. Empowered teams are more likely to embrace change and take ownership of the outcomes.

Section 2: Overcoming Resistance to Change
Resistance to change is natural, but leaders can take proactive steps to address it effectively:

1. Understand the concerns: Take the time to understand the reasons behind resistance. Listen actively to your team members' concerns, empathize with their perspectives, and address any misconceptions.

2. Communicate the benefits: Clearly articulate the benefits of the proposed change. Help your team members understand how the change aligns with the organization's goals, improves efficiency, or enhances their skills and professional growth.

3. Provide support: Offer support and resources to facilitate the transition. Provide training, coaching, and mentoring as needed to help your team members adapt to new processes, technologies, or ways of working.

4. Foster a culture of continuous learning: Encourage a growth mindset within your team. Emphasize the importance of learning, experimentation, and adapting to new challenges. Celebrate and reward innovation and creativity.

5. Address individual concerns: Some resistance may stem from individual fears or insecurities. Take the time to address these concerns on a personal level. Provide reassurance, guidance, or additional support as necessary.

Section 3: Building Resilience in Yourself and Your Team
Resilience is crucial for navigating change and uncertainty. Here's how leaders can foster resilience:

1. Cultivate self-awareness: Understand your own strengths, weaknesses, and triggers in the face of change. Develop coping strategies that work for you, such as practicing mindfulness, seeking support from mentors, or maintaining a healthy work-life balance.

2. Foster a supportive environment: Create a safe and supportive team culture where individuals feel comfortable expressing their concerns and seeking help. Encourage open dialogue, collaboration, and mutual support.

3. Encourage adaptability: Help your team members develop adaptability skills by encouraging them to step out of their comfort zones, take on new challenges, and learn

from setbacks. Provide opportunities for growth and skill development.

4. Celebrate resilience: Recognize and celebrate instances of resilience within your team. Acknowledge and reward individuals who demonstrate adaptability, perseverance, and innovative problem-solving.

5. Provide resources for well-being: Prioritize the well-being of your team members. Offer resources such as employee assistance programs, wellness initiatives, or flexible work arrangements to support their physical and mental health.

Conclusion:
Managing change and uncertainty is an essential leadership skill. By navigating change effectively, addressing resistance, and building resilience, leaders can help their teams thrive amidst uncertainty, foster a culture of growth, and achieve long-term success. Remember, change presents opportunities for growth and innovation, and it is through embracing these opportunities that leaders can make a lasting impact.

Chapter 10: Cultivating Innovation and Creativity

Introduction:
In today's rapidly changing world, innovation and creativity have become essential for organizations to stay competitive and thrive. This chapter will explore the importance of fostering a culture of innovation, encouraging creativity and risk-taking, and implementing ideas effectively.

1. Fostering a Culture of Innovation:
Creating an environment that nurtures innovation is crucial for generating new ideas and promoting creative problem-solving. Here are some key strategies:

a. Leadership support: Leaders should champion innovation and demonstrate their commitment to it. They need to communicate the importance of innovation, set clear expectations, and provide the necessary resources and support.

b. Open communication: Encourage open dialogue and collaboration among team members. This includes creating opportunities for brainstorming, sharing ideas, and providing feedback. Foster an inclusive culture where everyone feels comfortable contributing their unique perspectives.

c. Tolerance for failure: Encourage a mindset that views failures as learning opportunities. Emphasize that taking calculated risks is a necessary part of the innovation process. Celebrate both successes and failures to promote a culture of continuous learning.

d. Cross-functional collaboration: Break down silos and promote collaboration across different departments or teams. Encourage individuals with diverse backgrounds and skill sets to work together, as this can lead to innovative solutions and fresh perspectives.

2. Encouraging Creativity and Risk-Taking:
Creativity is the foundation of innovation, and organizations must create an environment that fosters and nurtures creative thinking. Here are some ways to encourage creativity and risk-taking:

a. Provide autonomy: Give employees the freedom to explore and experiment with their ideas. Encourage them to think outside the box and pursue unconventional approaches. Providing autonomy helps foster a sense of ownership and encourages individuals to take risks.

b. Remove barriers: Identify and eliminate any obstacles that hinder creativity. This could include outdated processes, excessive bureaucracy, or rigid hierarchies. Create a supportive environment where individuals feel empowered to challenge the status quo.

c. Encourage diverse perspectives: Diversity of thought is essential for creativity. Encourage employees to seek input from different sources, including colleagues, customers, and external experts. Embrace a culture that values and respects diverse viewpoints.

d. Provide resources and training: Invest in providing employees with the necessary tools, training, and resources to enhance their creativity and innovation skills. Offer workshops, training programs, or mentorship opportunities to develop these capabilities.

3. Implementing Ideas Effectively:
Even the most innovative ideas are meaningless if they are not effectively implemented. Here are some strategies for successful idea implementation:

a. Clear goals and metrics: Set clear objectives and key performance indicators (KPIs) for implementing innovative ideas. This helps measure progress, provides a sense of direction, and ensures alignment with the organization's overall strategy.

b. Adequate resources: Allocate the necessary resources, including funding, manpower, and time, to implement ideas effectively. Lack of resources can hinder the successful execution of even the best ideas.

c. Agile project management: Embrace agile project management methodologies that allow for flexibility and adaptability. Break down projects into smaller, manageable tasks and iterate as needed. Regularly review progress, make adjustments, and keep stakeholders informed.

d. Celebrate successes and learn from failures: Recognize and celebrate successful implementation of innovative ideas. This helps reinforce the importance of innovation and motivates others. Additionally, learn from failures and make improvements based on lessons learned.

Conclusion:
Cultivating a culture of innovation, encouraging creativity and risk-taking, and implementing ideas effectively are essential for organizations seeking to thrive in today's competitive landscape. By fostering an environment that values and supports innovation, organizations can unleash the full potential of their employees and drive sustainable growth and success.

Chapter 11: Strategic Thinking and Decision-Making

Section 1: Developing Strategic Thinking Skills

Strategic thinking is a critical skill for effective leadership and decision-making. It involves the ability to analyze complex situations, anticipate future trends, and formulate innovative approaches to achieve goals. Here are some key steps to develop strategic thinking skills:

1. Environmental Analysis: Stay updated on the external environment by monitoring industry trends, technological advancements, and market dynamics. Understand how these factors can impact your organization and its goals.

2. Systems Thinking: Embrace a holistic perspective by considering the interconnectedness of various elements within your organization and its ecosystem. Identify the relationships and dependencies between different parts of the system.

3. Long-term Vision: Develop a clear vision of what you want to achieve in the future. Define your organization's purpose, mission, and core values. This vision will serve as a guiding compass for strategic decision-making.

4. Critical Thinking: Enhance your analytical and problem-solving abilities. Challenge assumptions, think critically about information, and seek diverse perspectives. This

helps in identifying underlying issues and uncovering new opportunities.

5. Creativity and Innovation: Foster a culture of creativity and encourage innovative thinking. Generate new ideas, explore different possibilities, and encourage experimentation. Embrace calculated risk-taking to drive strategic growth.

Section 2: Evaluating Options and Making Informed Decisions

Strategic decision-making involves assessing various alternatives and selecting the most suitable option. Here are some steps to evaluate options and make informed decisions:

1. Define Decision Criteria: Clearly establish the criteria against which you will evaluate options. Consider factors like feasibility, impact on stakeholders, cost-effectiveness, and alignment with organizational goals.

2. Gather Relevant Information: Conduct thorough research and gather all pertinent data related to each option. This includes both quantitative and qualitative information. Consider input from subject matter experts and stakeholders.

3. Analyze and Compare Options: Systematically evaluate each option against the defined criteria. Use tools like SWOT (Strengths, Weaknesses, Opportunities, Threats)

analysis, decision matrices, and cost-benefit analysis to compare alternatives.

4. Scenario Planning: Anticipate different scenarios and assess how each option would perform under those circumstances. Consider potential risks, uncertainties, and future trends to make robust decisions that can withstand changing conditions.

5. Consultation and Collaboration: Seek input from relevant stakeholders and experts. Engage in discussions, brainstorming sessions, and debates to gain diverse perspectives and insights. This fosters better decision-making through collective intelligence.

Section 3: Balancing Short-term and Long-term Goals

Balancing short-term and long-term goals is essential for sustainable success. Here are some strategies to achieve this balance:

1. Clearly Define Objectives: Establish specific short-term and long-term goals that are aligned with your organization's vision and values. Ensure that the objectives are measurable and time-bound to track progress effectively.

2. Prioritize: Evaluate the urgency and importance of each goal. Identify which goals are critical for immediate success and which contribute to long-term growth. Allocate resources, accordingly, focusing on high-priority areas.

3. Strategic Alignment: Regularly assess how short-term actions align with long-term objectives. Ensure that short-term goals do not conflict with or compromise the attainment of long-term strategic goals.

4. Flexibility and Adaptability: Embrace agility and adaptability in your strategic approach. Recognize that circumstances may change, requiring adjustments to the balance between short-term and long-term goals. Be open to course corrections when necessary.

5. Communication and Engagement: Foster a shared understanding of the organization's short-term and long-term goals. Communicate the rationale behind decisions to build trust and commitment among stakeholders. Engage employees in the process, ensuring their understanding and buy-in.

Conclusion: By developing strategic thinking skills, evaluating options systematically, and balancing short-term and long-term goals, you can enhance your decision-making capabilities and lead your organization towards success in a dynamic business environment.

Chapter 12: Leading Through Crisis

Introduction:
Leading through crisis is a defining moment for any leader. During these challenging times, effective crisis management, clear communication, maintaining composure, and providing guidance are crucial for navigating uncertainty and leading your team towards resolution. In this chapter, we will explore key strategies and principles for handling crisis situations effectively, communicating during times of uncertainty, and maintaining composure while providing guidance.

Section 1: Handling Crisis Situations Effectively
1. Understanding the nature of the crisis:
   - Assessing the severity, impact, and potential consequences of the crisis.
   - Identifying the root causes and developing a comprehensive understanding of the situation.

2. Acting decisively and swiftly:
   - Establishing a crisis management team or task force to coordinate efforts.
   - Making prompt decisions based on the available information, while remaining flexible to adapt as the situation evolves.

3. Prioritizing and allocating resources:
   - Identifying critical areas requiring immediate attention.
   - Allocating resources efficiently to address those areas effectively.

- Anticipating and preparing for potential cascading effects of the crisis.

4. Communicating transparently:
   - Being open, honest, and transparent with your team, stakeholders, and the public.
   - Sharing relevant information about the crisis, its impacts, and the steps being taken to mitigate it.
   - Addressing concerns, providing reassurance, and managing expectations.

Section 2: Communicating During Times of Uncertainty
1. Establishing a communication plan:
   - Developing a clear and proactive communication strategy for different stages of the crisis.
   - Identifying key messages and adapting them to different audiences.
   - Utilizing various communication channels effectively (e.g., email, meetings, social media, press releases) to reach stakeholders.

2. Active listening and empathy:
   - Encouraging open dialogue and actively listening to the concerns and feedback of team members and stakeholders.
   - Demonstrating empathy and understanding for their emotions and perspectives.
   - Addressing concerns and providing support where possible.

3. Providing regular updates:
   - Keeping stakeholders informed about the progress of crisis management efforts.
   - Communicating updates frequently, even if there are no significant developments, to prevent speculation and rumors.
   - Clarifying any misinformation or misconceptions promptly.

Section 3: Maintaining Composure and Providing Guidance
1. Leading by example:
   - Demonstrating calmness, resilience, and confidence in the face of adversity.
   - Maintaining a positive attitude and projecting stability to inspire and motivate others.

2. Fostering a culture of trust:
   - Building trust with your team and stakeholders through consistent communication and transparency.
   - Encouraging open and honest discussions, even when the information is challenging or uncertain.

3. Providing clear direction:
   - Setting a clear vision and objectives for navigating the crisis.
   - Offering guidance on the steps to be taken and the roles and responsibilities of team members.
   - Adjusting plans as needed and communicating changes effectively.

4. Supporting the well-being of individuals:
   - Acknowledging the emotional impact of the crisis on individuals and teams.
   - Providing support, resources, and access to appropriate channels for seeking help or guidance.
   - Encouraging self-care and work-life balance during demanding times.

Conclusion:
Leading through crisis requires a combination of effective crisis management, transparent communication, maintaining composure, and providing guidance. By understanding the nature of the crisis, communicating transparently during uncertainty, and exhibiting leadership qualities, you can lead your team through challenging times and contribute to the successful resolution of the crisis.

Chapter 13: Inspiring and Motivating Others

Introduction:
Inspiring and motivating others is a crucial skill for any leader or individual in a position of influence. This chapter explores the art of inspiring others to take action and the various motivational techniques and strategies that can be employed. Additionally, it emphasizes the importance of recognizing and rewarding achievements as a means to foster motivation and encourage continued success.

Section 1: The Art of Inspiring Others to Action
1.1 Understanding the power of inspiration:
   - The impact of inspiration on individuals and teams
   - The role of a leader in inspiring others
   - Inspiring through personal example and storytelling

1.2 Communicating a compelling vision:
   - Developing a clear and inspiring vision
   - Aligning personal and organizational values
   - Effective communication techniques to convey the vision

1.3 Building trust and credibility:
   - The importance of trust in inspiring others
   - Developing credibility through competence and character
   - Establishing authentic connections with others

Section 2: Motivational Techniques and Strategies
2.1 Setting meaningful goals:

- The significance of goal setting in motivation
- SMART (Specific, Measurable, Achievable, Relevant, Time-bound) goal framework
- Involving others in goal setting for increased motivation

2.2 Providing constructive feedback and support:
- The role of feedback in motivating others
- Delivering feedback effectively and constructively
- Offering support and resources to facilitate success

2.3 Encouraging autonomy and empowerment:
- Empowering others to take ownership of their work
- Granting autonomy within established boundaries
- Enabling creativity and innovation

Section 3: Recognizing and Rewarding Achievements
3.1 Importance of recognition and rewards:
- The psychological impact of recognition and rewards
- Linking achievements to organizational goals and values
- Enhancing job satisfaction and engagement through recognition

3.2 Implementing effective recognition strategies:
- Tailoring recognition to individual preferences
- Public vs. private recognition
- Creating a culture of appreciation and celebration

3.3 non-monetary and intrinsic rewards:
- Identifying non-monetary rewards and incentives
- Tapping into intrinsic motivation factors
- Providing opportunities for growth and development

Conclusion:

Inspiring and motivating others is an ongoing process that requires understanding human psychology, effective communication, and strategic implementation of various techniques. By mastering the art of inspiration, employing motivational strategies, and recognizing achievements, individuals can cultivate a motivated and engaged workforce, resulting in increased productivity, satisfaction, and overall success.

Chapter 14: Mentoring and Developing Others

Introduction:
Mentoring plays a vital role in leadership by facilitating the growth and development of individuals within an organization. In this chapter, we will explore the importance of mentoring, nurturing talent, fostering growth, and providing constructive feedback and support to mentees. Effective mentoring can have a significant impact on both the mentee and the mentor, contributing to the overall success of the organization.

Section 1: The Importance of Mentoring in Leadership

Mentoring is an essential component of effective leadership for several reasons. Firstly, it promotes knowledge sharing and transfer, allowing experienced leaders to pass on their expertise and wisdom to the next generation of leaders. Mentoring enables the preservation of institutional knowledge and helps avoid reinventing the wheel. Additionally, it creates a supportive environment that encourages learning, growth, and innovation within the organization. By investing in the development of others, leaders can enhance the overall capabilities and performance of their team.

Section 2: Nurturing Talent and Fostering Growth

Mentoring provides an opportunity to identify and nurture talent within an organization. Effective mentors recognize the potential in their mentees and actively support their growth. They provide guidance, resources, and opportunities for mentees to expand their skills, knowledge, and experience. Mentors also help mentees set challenging goals and encourage them to step out of their comfort zones. By fostering growth in their mentees, leaders contribute to the long-term success of their teams and the organization as a whole.

Section 3: Providing Constructive Feedback and Support
Constructive feedback is a crucial aspect of mentoring. Effective mentors provide timely and specific feedback to their mentees, highlighting areas of improvement and offering guidance on how to enhance performance. They focus on the mentee's strengths and weaknesses, helping them build on their strengths while addressing areas that need development. Moreover, mentors provide emotional support and create a safe space for mentees to share their challenges, concerns, and aspirations. By offering support, mentors build trust and rapport with their mentees, fostering a positive mentoring relationship.

Conclusion:
Mentoring is an invaluable tool for leadership development and organizational success. By embracing the role of mentor, leaders can nurture talent, foster growth, and provide constructive feedback and support to their mentees. Effective mentoring creates a culture of continuous learning and development, leading to higher employee engagement, increased productivity, and improved retention rates. Ultimately, investing in mentoring and developing others not only benefits individual mentees but also contributes to the long-term success and sustainability of the organization.

Chapter 15: Influencing and Negotiating

Introduction:
In today's complex and interconnected world, effective leaders must possess influential leadership skills, master negotiation techniques, and establish strategic alliances and partnerships. This chapter will explore these three essential aspects of leadership and provide practical insights on developing and applying them successfully.

Section 1: Developing Influential Leadership Skills
1. Understanding influential leadership:
   - Definition and importance of influential leadership.
   - Key attributes of influential leaders: charisma, credibility, and emotional intelligence.
   - The role of trust and integrity in influential leadership.

2. Building personal credibility:
   - Developing expertise and knowledge in relevant areas.
   - Demonstrating consistency in actions and words.
   - Building a positive reputation through ethical conduct.

3. Enhancing communication skills:
   - Active listening and empathetic understanding.
   - Effective verbal and nonverbal communication.
   - Tailoring messages to different audiences.

4. Leveraging emotional intelligence:
   - Understanding and managing emotions.
   - Empathy and its role in influencing others.
   - Building strong relationships and rapport.

Section 2: Effective Negotiation Techniques

1. Understanding negotiation:
   - Definition and importance of negotiation skills.
   - Different types of negotiation: distributive and integrative.

2. Preparation and planning:
   - Setting clear goals and objectives.
   - Gathering relevant information and understanding the other party's perspective.
   - Identifying possible concessions and alternatives.

3. Building rapport and trust:
   - Creating a positive and collaborative atmosphere.
   - Active listening and demonstrating understanding.
   - Finding common ground and shared interests.

4. Communication and persuasion:
   - Effective communication strategies during negotiation.
   - Framing messages and using persuasive techniques.
   - Managing conflicts and resolving disagreements.

5. Win-win solutions and creative problem-solving:
   - Exploring options and generating alternatives.
   - Seeking mutually beneficial outcomes.
   - Overcoming impasses and finding innovative solutions.

Section 3: Building Strategic Alliances and Partnerships

1. Understanding strategic alliances and partnerships:
   - Definition and benefits of forming strategic alliances.
   - Different types of alliances: joint ventures, licensing, and co-branding.

2. Identifying potential partners:
   - Assessing compatibility and shared goals.
   - Evaluating complementary strengths and resources.
   - Conducting due diligence and background research.

3. Negotiating and structuring partnerships:
   - Establishing clear objectives and expectations.
   - Drafting comprehensive agreements and contracts.
   - Defining roles, responsibilities, and decision-making processes.

4. Managing and nurturing partnerships:
   - Building trust and effective communication channels.
   - Resolving conflicts and addressing challenges.
   - Continuous evaluation and adapting to changing circumstances.

Conclusion:

Developing influential leadership skills, mastering effective negotiation techniques, and building strategic alliances and partnerships are crucial for leaders seeking success in today's dynamic environment. By cultivating these skills and applying them strategically, leaders can positively influence others, negotiate win-win outcomes, and forge valuable collaborations that drive organizational growth and success.

Chapter 16: Managing Time and Priorities

Introduction:
Effective time management and prioritization are crucial skills for leaders. In this chapter, we will explore various strategies and techniques that can help leaders manage their time more efficiently, prioritize tasks and responsibilities effectively, and delegate tasks to others in a way that maximizes productivity and achieves organizational goals.

1. Time Management Strategies for Leaders:
Time management is all about making the best use of available time and resources. Here are some strategies that leaders can employ to enhance their time management skills:

a. Planning and Goal Setting: Leaders should establish clear goals and objectives and create a roadmap for achieving them. This enables them to focus on tasks that align with their overall vision and mission.

b. Prioritization: It is essential to identify and prioritize tasks based on their importance and urgency. Leaders should categorize tasks into four quadrants: urgent and important, important but not urgent, urgent but not important, and not urgent and not important. This helps in determining where to allocate time and resources.

c. Time Blocking: Allocating specific time blocks for different tasks or activities can improve productivity.

Leaders can schedule uninterrupted blocks of time for important tasks, meetings, and strategic thinking.

d. Avoiding Procrastination: Leaders must recognize and address procrastination tendencies. Breaking tasks into smaller, manageable parts and setting deadlines can help overcome procrastination.

e. Limiting Distractions: Distractions can significantly impact productivity. Leaders should identify and minimize distractions such as unnecessary meetings, excessive email checking, or social media usage during focused work periods.

f. Leveraging Technology: Utilize productivity tools, project management software, and calendar apps to streamline workflow, automate routine tasks, and stay organized.

2. Prioritizing Tasks and Responsibilities:
Prioritization involves identifying and focusing on the most important tasks that align with strategic objectives. Here are some steps leaders can follow to prioritize effectively:

a. Assessing Importance and Urgency: Evaluate tasks based on their impact on organizational goals and deadlines. Consider the consequences of not completing certain tasks on time.

b. Alignment with Strategic Goals: Determine how each task contributes to the overall mission and vision of the organization. Prioritize tasks that align closely with strategic objectives.

c. Considering Dependencies: Identify tasks that are dependent on the completion of other tasks or require input from others. Prioritize tasks that unblock dependencies or enable progress on critical projects.

d. Time and Resource Constraints: Take into account the time and resources required to complete tasks. Consider the availability and capacity of resources to allocate them effectively.

e. Flexibility and Adaptability: Priorities may change as new information or opportunities arise. Leaders should be open to adjusting priorities when necessary and communicate changes effectively.

3. Delegating Effectively:
Delegation is a vital skill for leaders to leverage the capabilities of their team members and focus on high-level tasks. Here are some key aspects of effective delegation:

a. Understanding Strengths and Skills: Assess the strengths, skills, and expertise of team members to assign tasks that match their abilities. This boosts productivity and employee engagement.

b. Clear Communication: Clearly communicate expectations, goals, and deadlines when delegating tasks.

Provide necessary resources, information, and support to ensure successful completion.

c. Empowering and Trusting Others: Delegate authority and responsibility to team members, allowing them to make decisions and take ownership of their tasks. Trust their abilities and provide guidance when needed.

d. Regular Follow-up and Feedback: Maintain regular communication and follow-up to track progress, provide feedback, and offer assistance if required. This ensures accountability and keeps tasks on track.

e. Learning from Delegation: Delegation is not only about task completion but also about professional growth. Encourage team members to share lessons learned and provide feedback on the delegation process.

Conclusion:
Managing time and priorities effectively is essential for leaders to optimize productivity and achieve organizational goals. By implementing time management strategies, prioritizing tasks and responsibilities, and delegating effectively, leaders can enhance their efficiency, leverage their team's capabilities, and focus on strategic initiatives that drive success.

Chapter 17: Leading with Resilience

Introduction:
In today's fast-paced and unpredictable business environment, leaders need to possess a crucial attribute: resilience. Resilience refers to the ability to bounce back from setbacks, adapt to change, and maintain a positive mindset in the face of adversity. In this chapter, we will explore the role of resilience in leadership and discuss strategies for managing stress and adversity. Additionally, we will delve into the process of bouncing back from setbacks, highlighting the importance of learning and growth in leadership development.

The Role of Resilience in Leadership:
Resilience is a vital quality for leaders as they navigate the challenges and complexities of their roles. Here are some key aspects of resilience that make it indispensable for effective leadership:

1. Emotional Stability: Leaders who are emotionally resilient can manage their own emotions during stressful situations, inspiring confidence and stability in their teams. They remain composed, make rational decisions, and maintain a positive outlook even in the face of adversity.

2. Adaptability: Resilient leaders embrace change and uncertainty. They are quick to adapt their strategies, priorities, and plans when circumstances require it. By fostering an agile and flexible mindset within their teams, they can navigate challenges and seize new opportunities.

3. Role Modeling: Resilient leaders serve as role models for their teams. Their ability to face setbacks head-on and persevere through difficult times inspires and motivates others to do the same. They demonstrate that resilience is not only a personal attribute but also a vital skill for success.

Strategies for Managing Stress and Adversity:
Leaders can employ various strategies to effectively manage stress and adversity, promoting resilience within themselves and their teams:

1. Self-Care: Prioritize self-care by maintaining a healthy work-life balance, exercising regularly, getting enough sleep, and engaging in activities that help you relax and recharge. Taking care of your physical and mental well-being enhances your ability to handle stress.

2. Building Support Networks: Cultivate strong support networks, both within and outside the workplace. Surround yourself with trusted colleagues, mentors, friends, or family members who can provide guidance, advice, and a listening ear during challenging times.

3. Practicing Mindfulness: Incorporate mindfulness practices into your daily routine, such as meditation, deep breathing exercises, or reflective journaling. Mindfulness helps you stay present, manage stress, and develop a clearer perspective on setbacks.

4. Effective Time Management: Develop efficient time management skills to prioritize tasks, delegate when necessary, and maintain a sense of control over your workload. Effective time management minimizes stress and allows you to focus on critical matters.

Bouncing Back from Setbacks:
Leaders inevitably encounter setbacks throughout their careers. Bouncing back from these setbacks requires a resilient mindset and proactive approach:

1. Reflection and Learning: Take the time to reflect on setbacks and identify the lessons they offer. What went wrong, and what can be learned from the experience? Encourage your team to engage in a similar reflection process, promoting a growth mindset within the organization.

2. Seeking Support: Reach out to your support network for guidance and advice when faced with setbacks. Utilize the collective knowledge and experience of trusted individuals to gain new perspectives and identify potential solutions.

3. Adjusting Strategies: Use the insights gained from setbacks to adjust your strategies and plans. A resilient leader is willing to reassess their approach and make necessary changes to overcome obstacles.

4. Maintaining Optimism: Stay positive and maintain a sense of optimism even in the face of setbacks. Communicate your belief in the team's ability to overcome challenges and emphasize the lessons learned from setbacks as opportunities for growth and improvement.

Conclusion:
Leading with resilience is a critical aspect of effective leadership. By embodying resilience, leaders can manage stress and adversity, inspire their teams, and navigate setbacks with grace.

Chapter 18: Embracing Diversity and Inclusion

Introduction:
In today's rapidly evolving and interconnected world, organizations must recognize the value of diversity and inclusion in fostering innovation, driving success, and creating a positive work environment. This chapter explores the importance of diversity in leadership, strategies for creating an inclusive and equitable workplace, and the ways in which organizations can leverage diversity to fuel innovation and achieve long-term success.

1. The Value of Diversity in Leadership:
1.1. Enhanced Decision-Making: Diverse leadership teams bring together individuals with varied perspectives, backgrounds, and experiences. This diversity of thought enables more comprehensive and informed decision-making processes, leading to better outcomes and mitigating the risks of groupthink.
1.2. Broader Representation: Having diverse leaders allows organizations to reflect the diverse customer base they serve. It enhances the ability to understand and cater to the needs of different demographic segments, resulting in improved customer satisfaction and loyalty.
1.3. Increased Creativity and Innovation: Diverse leadership fosters an environment that encourages the exchange of ideas and promotes creativity. Different perspectives and approaches spark innovative thinking, leading to the development of novel solutions and products.

2. Creating an Inclusive and Equitable Environment:

2.1. Dismantling Bias: Organizations must actively address biases, both explicit and implicit, that hinder inclusivity. This involves implementing bias training programs, establishing unbiased hiring and promotion practices, and promoting a culture of respect and fairness.

2.2. Building Cultural Competence: Organizations should invest in training and development initiatives that help employees understand and appreciate different cultures, backgrounds, and perspectives. This cultivates empathy, reduces stereotypes, and creates a more inclusive environment.

2.3. Employee Resource Groups: Establishing employee resource groups (ERGs) provides a platform for underrepresented individuals to connect, share experiences, and contribute to shaping an inclusive workplace. ERGs can also act as valuable sources of feedback for organizational policies and practices.

3. Leveraging Diversity for Innovation and Success:

3.1. Collaboration and Teamwork: Embracing diversity in teams fosters collaboration, leading to richer discussions, increased creativity, and improved problem-solving. Diverse teams are more likely to identify a wider range of solutions and make better-informed decisions.

3.2. Market Opportunities: Diversity in the workforce enables organizations to understand and tap into new market segments. Diverse perspectives help identify unmet needs, allowing for the development of products and services that cater to a broader customer base.

3.3. Employee Engagement and Retention: A diverse and inclusive workplace promotes employee engagement and fosters a sense of belonging. When employees feel valued and respected, they are more likely to be loyal, motivated, and committed to the organization's success.

Conclusion:
Embracing diversity and inclusion is not only a moral imperative but also a strategic advantage for organizations. By recognizing the value of diversity in leadership, creating an inclusive and equitable environment, and leveraging diversity for innovation and success, organizations can unlock the full potential of their workforce, drive innovation, and establish a competitive edge in the global marketplace.

Chapter 19: Leading in a Global Context

Introduction:
In today's interconnected world, leaders are faced with the challenges and opportunities of operating in a globalized context. This chapter explores the key aspects of leading in a global context, including understanding the challenges and opportunities, developing cross-cultural competencies, and building effective virtual teams. By mastering these skills, leaders can navigate the complexities of global leadership and create successful outcomes in diverse environments.

1. Understanding the Challenges and Opportunities of Leading in a Globalized World:
In this section, we delve into the unique challenges and opportunities that leaders encounter in a globalized world. Globalization has brought diverse cultures, markets, and perspectives closer together, presenting leaders with a range of complexities. Some challenges include:

a. Cultural differences: Leaders must understand and navigate cultural differences to build strong relationships and effective teams. This involves recognizing varying communication styles, norms, values, and expectations across cultures.

b. Geographical dispersion: Leading global teams often means dealing with geographical dispersion, with team members spread across different time zones and locations.

Leaders need to find ways to overcome these challenges and create a sense of unity and collaboration.

c. Legal and regulatory complexities: Operating in different countries means leaders must navigate diverse legal and regulatory frameworks. Understanding and complying with various laws and regulations is crucial to avoid legal issues and maintain ethical practices.

However, leading in a globalized world also presents numerous opportunities, such as:

a. Access to diverse talent: Globalization allows leaders to tap into a wider pool of talent with diverse skills, experiences, and perspectives. This can enhance innovation, creativity, and problem-solving within organizations.

b. Expanded markets: Global leaders have the opportunity to expand their organizations' reach into new markets and customer segments. By understanding local markets and adapting strategies accordingly, leaders can capitalize on new growth opportunities.

2. Developing Cross-Cultural Competencies:
To lead effectively in a global context, leaders must develop cross-cultural competencies. These competencies enable leaders to understand and adapt to different cultural norms, values, and behaviors. Key considerations for developing cross-cultural competencies include:

a. Cultural intelligence (CQ): Cultural intelligence involves understanding cultural differences, adapting behaviors, and effectively interacting with individuals from different backgrounds. Leaders can enhance their CQ through training, exposure to diverse cultures, and building relationships with people from various backgrounds.

b. Empathy and cultural sensitivity: Leaders must cultivate empathy and cultural sensitivity to appreciate and respect diverse perspectives. This includes actively listening, seeking feedback, and demonstrating openness to different viewpoints.

c. Communication and language skills: Effective communication is crucial in a global context. Leaders should strive to enhance their communication skills, including cross-cultural communication and the ability to bridge language barriers. This may involve learning languages or leveraging translation and interpretation resources.

3. Building Effective Virtual Teams:
Virtual teams are increasingly prevalent in a globalized world, bringing together individuals who work remotely or are geographically dispersed. Leaders must develop strategies to build and manage effective virtual teams. Considerations for building effective virtual teams include:

a. Clear goals and expectations: Leaders should establish clear goals, roles, and expectations to ensure team members are aligned and understand their responsibilities.

This clarity promotes accountability and enhances team performance.

b. Leveraging technology: Effective use of technology tools and platforms can foster collaboration, communication, and knowledge sharing within virtual teams. Leaders should identify and implement appropriate technologies that facilitate seamless virtual teamwork.

c. Building trust and rapport: Trust is vital for virtual teams to function effectively. Leaders should foster trust through regular communication, providing support, recognizing achievements, and creating opportunities for virtual team members to bond and build relationships.

Conclusion:
Leading in a global context requires leaders to embrace the challenges and opportunities presented by globalization. By understanding these challenges, developing cross-cultural competencies, and building effective virtual teams, leaders can navigate.

Chapter 20: Balancing Work and Life

Introduction:
In today's fast-paced and demanding work environment, achieving a healthy work-life balance is crucial for both leaders and their teams. As a leader, it is essential to manage your personal well-being and create a supportive environment that encourages work-life balance for your team members. This chapter will explore strategies for achieving work-life balance as a leader, managing personal well-being, and fostering a supportive work environment for your team.

Section 1: Achieving Work-Life Balance as a Leader
1. Recognize the importance of work-life balance: Understand that maintaining a healthy work-life balance is vital not only for your well-being but also for your effectiveness as a leader.
2. Set clear boundaries: Clearly define your working hours and communicate them to your team. Avoid overworking and establish a healthy separation between work and personal life.
3. Delegate and empower your team: Trust your team members and delegate tasks accordingly. Empowering your team allows you to focus on essential leadership responsibilities and creates a sense of shared ownership.
4. Prioritize tasks: Practice effective time management by prioritizing tasks and focusing on high-value activities. This helps prevent burnout and ensures that you dedicate time to both work and personal commitments.

5. Utilize technology effectively: Leverage technology tools to streamline work processes, automate repetitive tasks, and improve efficiency. Embrace tools that promote flexible work arrangements and remote collaboration.

Section 2: Managing Personal Well-being and Self-Care

1. Maintain a healthy lifestyle: Prioritize regular exercise, a balanced diet, and sufficient sleep. These habits contribute to your overall well-being and enhance your ability to handle work challenges effectively.
2. Practice mindfulness and stress management: Incorporate mindfulness techniques, such as meditation or deep breathing exercises, into your daily routine to reduce stress and promote mental clarity.
3. Set aside personal time: Dedicate regular time to engage in activities that bring you joy and relaxation. Whether it's pursuing a hobby, spending time with loved ones, or engaging in self-care practices, make personal time a priority.
4. Seek support: Don't hesitate to reach out to mentors, peers, or support networks for guidance and encouragement. Surround yourself with a support system that understands the demands of leadership and provides a safe space for sharing challenges and seeking advice.

Section 3: Creating a Supportive Environment for Your Team

1. Lead by example: Model work-life balance by practicing what you preach. Demonstrate healthy work habits, take time off when needed, and openly communicate the importance of work-life balance to your team.

2. Foster open communication: Encourage transparent and open communication within your team. Create a safe space for team members to discuss their work-life challenges and provide support or accommodations when possible.

3. Offer flexible work arrangements: Where feasible, provide flexible work options such as remote work, flexible hours, or compressed workweeks. This allows team members to balance their personal and professional commitments more effectively.

4. Set realistic expectations: Ensure that your team's workload and deadlines are reasonable and achievable. Avoid overloading individuals with excessive work, as it can lead to stress and hamper work-life balance.

5. Support professional development: Invest in your team's growth and development by providing opportunities for training and upskilling. This demonstrates your commitment to their long-term success and reinforces a culture that values work-life balance.

Conclusion:

Achieving work-life balance as a leader requires conscious effort and commitment. By prioritizing work-life balance for yourself and creating a supportive environment for your team, you can enhance productivity, well-being, and overall job satisfaction. Remember, a balanced and fulfilled leader sets the stage for a motivated and engaged team.

Chapter 21: Nurturing Continuous Learning

Introduction:
In today's rapidly evolving world, where new technologies, ideas, and paradigms emerge constantly, it is essential for leaders to embrace lifelong learning. Continuous learning not only enhances personal growth and development but also equips leaders with the knowledge and skills necessary to navigate challenges and drive success in their organizations. In this chapter, we will explore the importance of lifelong learning in leadership, how to develop a personal learning plan, and strategies to encourage a culture of learning within your organization.

1. The Importance of Lifelong Learning in Leadership:
Leadership is no longer solely about possessing expertise and experience; it requires adaptability, innovation, and the ability to stay ahead of the curve. Lifelong learning enables leaders to:

a. Stay Relevant: Lifelong learning ensures leaders stay up to date with the latest trends, technologies, and industry developments, enabling them to make informed decisions.

b. Enhance Problem-Solving Abilities: Continuous learning expands leaders' knowledge base and equips them with diverse perspectives, enabling them to approach problem-solving from various angles and make more effective decisions.

c. Foster Innovation: Learning fosters creativity and innovation by exposing leaders to new ideas and alternative ways of thinking. It encourages experimentation and helps leaders develop the agility needed to adapt to changing circumstances.

d. Embrace Change: In a dynamic business environment, change is inevitable. Lifelong learning helps leaders embrace change, overcome resistance, and lead their teams through transitions effectively.

e. Inspire and Motivate Others: Leaders who demonstrate a commitment to learning inspire their teams to do the same. By modeling a growth mindset and sharing their knowledge, leaders foster a culture of learning and encourage personal and professional development among their employees.

2. Developing a Personal Learning Plan:
To make lifelong learning a deliberate and structured practice, leaders can create a personal learning plan. Here are some steps to consider:

a. Set Learning Goals: Identify areas of knowledge and skills you want to develop. Reflect on your current strengths and weaknesses and define clear, achievable learning goals aligned with your personal and professional aspirations.

b. Identify Learning Opportunities: Explore various learning resources, such as books, articles, podcasts, webinars, workshops, online courses, and conferences. Consider both formal and informal avenues that suit your learning style and schedule.

c. Create a Learning Schedule: Allocate dedicated time for learning activities in your schedule. Treat it as a priority and establish a routine to ensure consistent progress.

d. Seek Diverse Perspectives: Engage with individuals from diverse backgrounds and industries to gain fresh perspectives. Join professional networks, attend industry events, and participate in mentorship programs to broaden your horizons.

e. Reflect and Apply Learning: Regularly reflect on your learning experiences and how they apply to your role as a leader. Integrate newfound knowledge into your decision-making process and share insights with your team to foster a culture of learning.

3. Encouraging a Culture of Learning in Your Organization: As a leader, you have the power to influence and shape the culture of your organization. Here are some strategies to foster a culture of learning:

a. Lead by Example: Demonstrate your commitment to continuous learning by sharing your learning experiences and encouraging others to do the same. Embrace feedback and be open to new ideas.

b. Provide Learning Opportunities: Invest in training and development programs that address the specific needs of your employees. Support their participation in conferences, workshops, and relevant courses. Encourage cross-functional collaboration to promote knowledge-sharing.

c. Promote a Growth Mindset: Foster an environment where mistakes are seen as learning opportunities rather than failures. Encourage employees to take risks, experiment, and learn from both successes and setbacks.

d. Establish Learning Communities: Encourage the formation of learning communities within your organization. This could involve regular knowledge.

-sharing sessions, book clubs, or mentoring programs, creating a supportive environment for ongoing learning and collaboration.

e. Recognize and Reward Learning: Acknowledge and reward employees who actively pursue learning and demonstrate the application of their knowledge to improve their work and contribute to the organization's goals.

Conclusion:

Nurturing continuous learning is an essential aspect of leadership in the modern world. By embracing lifelong learning, developing a personal learning plan, and fostering a culture of learning within your organization, you can enhance your leadership capabilities, drive innovation, and empower your team to thrive in an ever-changing environment. Remember, the journey of learning is ongoing, and as a leader, your commitment to growth and development will inspire and motivate others to do the same.

Chapter 22: Leading with Authenticity

Introduction:
In today's complex and ever-changing business landscape, authentic leadership has emerged as a powerful approach to inspire and motivate teams. Authentic leaders are those who embrace their true selves, align their values with their actions, and build trust through genuine leadership. In this chapter, we will explore the significance of authenticity in leadership, discuss the importance of aligning values with actions, and examine how authentic leaders can build trust within their teams.

1. Embracing authenticity in leadership:
Authenticity in leadership refers to being true to oneself and leading from a place of genuineness. Authentic leaders are aware of their strengths, weaknesses, and values, and they are not afraid to show vulnerability. By embracing authenticity, leaders create an environment where team members feel comfortable being themselves, leading to increased engagement, creativity, and productivity. Authentic leaders inspire trust and foster stronger relationships within their teams.

2. Aligning your values with your actions:
One of the essential aspects of authentic leadership is aligning personal values with actions. It is not enough to merely talk about values; authentic leaders demonstrate their commitment through consistent behavior. When leaders align their actions with their stated values, they create a sense of integrity and credibility. This alignment

also helps in decision-making processes, as leaders can rely on their core values to guide them through difficult choices.

3. Building trust through genuine leadership:
Trust is the foundation of any successful team or organization. Authentic leaders build trust by consistently displaying honesty, transparency, and integrity. They communicate openly, admit mistakes when they occur, and seek feedback from their team members. By being genuine in their interactions, authentic leaders create an environment where trust can flourish. Trust enables teams to collaborate effectively, take risks, and achieve exceptional results.

Conclusion:
Authentic leadership is a powerful approach that enables leaders to connect with their teams on a deeper level. By embracing authenticity, aligning their values with actions, and building trust, leaders can create an environment where individuals thrive, relationships strengthen, and organizations succeed. In the fast-paced and competitive business world, authentic leadership is a key differentiator that inspires loyalty, engagement, and innovation. Aspiring leaders should strive to lead with authenticity to make a meaningful and lasting impact on their teams and organizations.

Chapter 23: Managing Stakeholder Relationships

Introduction:
Managing stakeholder relationships is crucial for the success of any project or initiative. Stakeholders are individuals or groups who have an interest or are affected by the outcome of a project. Engaging and managing key stakeholders effectively is essential to ensure their support, involvement, and satisfaction throughout the project lifecycle. In this chapter, we will explore stakeholder analysis, communication strategies, and the importance of building partnerships for successful project outcomes.

1. Stakeholder Analysis:
Stakeholder analysis is the process of identifying and assessing the interests, expectations, and influence of various stakeholders. It involves identifying key stakeholders, understanding their needs, concerns, and objectives, and evaluating their level of influence and potential impact on the project. By conducting a stakeholder analysis, project managers can prioritize stakeholders and develop tailored strategies to engage and manage them effectively.

2. Engaging and Managing Key Stakeholders:
Engaging and managing key stakeholders involves establishing and maintaining effective communication channels and building relationships based on trust, transparency, and mutual understanding. Some key considerations for engaging and managing stakeholders include:

a. Identifying stakeholders: Identify all relevant stakeholders, both internal and external to the organization, who have an interest in or are impacted by the project.

b. Understanding stakeholder interests: Determine the key interests, concerns, and objectives of each stakeholder. This understanding will help in aligning project goals and addressing potential conflicts.

c. Communication strategies: Develop a communication plan that outlines the frequency, format, and content of communication with stakeholders. Different stakeholders may require different communication approaches.

d. Building trust and credibility: Establish trust by delivering on commitments, providing accurate and timely information, and involving stakeholders in decision-making processes where appropriate.

e. Addressing concerns and conflicts: Actively listen to stakeholders' concerns and address them promptly. Anticipate and manage conflicts that may arise due to differing stakeholder interests.

f. Seeking stakeholder input: Involve stakeholders in project planning and decision-making processes to gather their input and incorporate their perspectives.

g. Monitoring stakeholder satisfaction: Regularly assess stakeholder satisfaction and adjust engagement strategies as needed. Feedback mechanisms, surveys, and regular check-ins can be used for this purpose.

3. Communication Strategies:
Effective communication is a critical aspect of stakeholder management. Communication strategies should be tailored to the needs and preferences of different stakeholders. Consider the following approaches:

a. Clear and concise messaging: Ensure that project information is communicated in a clear, concise, and jargon-free manner to facilitate understanding.

b. Two-way communication: Encourage open dialogue and feedback from stakeholders. Actively listen to their concerns and suggestions and provide timely responses.

c. Use of appropriate channels: Utilize various communication channels such as meetings, emails, newsletters, social media, and project portals to reach stakeholders effectively.

d. Regular updates: Provide regular updates on project progress, milestones, and any changes that may impact stakeholders. Transparency helps build trust and keeps stakeholders engaged.

e. Tailored communication: Adapt communication styles and formats to suit the preferences and needs of different stakeholders. Some may prefer detailed reports, while others may prefer visual presentations or face-to-face meetings.

4. Building Partnerships for Success:
Building partnerships with stakeholders can enhance project success and sustainability. Partnerships involve collaborative relationships based on shared goals and mutual benefits. Consider the following approaches:

   a. Identifying partnership opportunities: Identify stakeholders who can contribute expertise, resources, or support to the project. Look for win-win scenarios where both parties benefit from the partnership.

   b. Developing formal agreements: Establish formal agreements or Memorandums of Understanding (MOUs) that outline the roles, responsibilities, and benefits of each partner. This helps set clear expectations and ensures commitment.

   c. Collaboration and shared decision-making: Foster a collaborative environment where stakeholders actively participate in decision-making processes. Encourage the sharing of ideas and perspectives to drive innovation and ownership.

   d. Recognizing and celebrating success: Acknowledge and celebrate the achievements of stakeholders and partnerships. This reinforces positive relationships and encourages continued collaboration.

e. Continuous engagement: Maintain regular communication and engagement with partners throughout the project lifecycle. Collaboration should extend beyond the project's completion to build long-term relationships.

Conclusion:
Effectively managing stakeholder relationships is vital for project success. Stakeholder analysis helps identify key stakeholders and understand their needs and expectations. By engaging stakeholders through tailored communication strategies, building trust, addressing concerns, and seeking their input, project managers can ensure stakeholder satisfaction and support. Additionally, building partnerships with stakeholders fosters collaboration, enhances project outcomes, and establishes a foundation for future success.

Chapter 24: Leveraging Technology for Leadership

Introduction:
In today's rapidly evolving digital age, leaders must adapt and leverage technology to stay ahead and effectively lead their teams. This chapter explores the importance of harnessing technology for leadership effectiveness, utilizing digital tools for communication and collaboration, and staying informed about emerging technologies.

Section 1: Harnessing technology for leadership effectiveness
1.1 Understanding the role of technology in leadership:
   - Technology as an enabler: How technology can enhance leadership capabilities and effectiveness.
   - Adapting to changing work environments: Leveraging technology to navigate remote work, virtual teams, and global collaborations.
   - Fostering innovation: Utilizing technology to encourage creativity, experimentation, and continuous improvement.

1.2 Enhancing decision-making with technology:
   - Data-driven leadership: Leveraging analytics and insights to make informed decisions.
   - Automation and AI: Harnessing artificial intelligence and automation to streamline processes and improve efficiency.
   - Predictive modeling: Using technology to forecast trends and anticipate future challenges.

1.3 Embracing digital transformation:
   - Leading organizational change: Using technology as a catalyst for driving digital transformation within the organization.
   - Developing a digital mindset: Cultivating a culture that embraces technological advancements and encourages digital fluency.
   - Overcoming resistance to change: Addressing challenges and promoting acceptance of new technologies among team members.

Section 2: Using digital tools for communication and collaboration.
2.1 Effective virtual communication:
   - Virtual meetings and conferences: Leveraging video conferencing tools for seamless communication and collaboration.
   - Remote team management: Techniques for managing and leading remote teams using digital communication channels.
   - Building rapport and trust: Strategies for fostering meaningful connections in a digital environment.

2.2 Collaboration platforms and project management tools:
   - Leveraging collaborative tools: Exploring project management software, team collaboration platforms, and knowledge-sharing systems.
   - Facilitating teamwork and coordination: Promoting collaboration, document sharing, and real-time updates using digital tools.

- Tracking progress and accountability: Monitoring team performance and progress through digital project management solutions.

2.3 Enhancing knowledge sharing and learning:
   - Online learning platforms: Utilizing e-learning platforms and virtual training programs to upskill team members.
   - Knowledge management systems: Leveraging digital repositories and knowledge-sharing platforms for efficient knowledge transfer.
   - Encouraging continuous learning: Creating a culture of continuous learning and professional development through digital resources.

Section 3: Staying informed about emerging technologies.
3.1 Monitoring technology trends:
   - Industry research and publications: Leveraging technology-focused publications and research to stay updated.
   - Attending conferences and seminars: Participating in relevant industry events to gain insights into emerging technologies.
   - Networking with technology professionals: Engaging with experts and peers to exchange knowledge and share insights.

3.2 Assessing the impact of emerging technologies:
   - Evaluating relevance and applicability: Determining how emerging technologies can benefit the organization's goals and strategies.

- Risk assessment and mitigation: Identifying potential risks and challenges associated with adopting new technologies.
  - Return on investment analysis: Assessing the potential benefits and ROI of implementing emerging technologies.

3.3 Developing a technology roadmap:
  - Aligning technology with organizational objectives: Developing a roadmap that integrates emerging technologies into the overall business strategy.
  - Prioritizing technology investments: Identifying key areas where technology can have the most significant impact and allocating resources accordingly.
  - Agile implementation: Embracing iterative and agile approaches to implement new technologies effectively.

Conclusion:
Leveraging technology for leadership effectiveness is essential in the digital era. Leaders must understand the role of technology in their leadership practices, effectively use digital tools for communication and collaboration, and stay informed about emerging technologies to drive innovation and success. By embracing technology and continuously adapting to its advancements, leaders can unlock new opportunities and lead their teams to thrive in a digital world.

Chapter 25: Reflecting and Evolving as a Leader

Introduction:
Leadership is not a static role; it requires constant growth and development. As a leader, it is essential to engage in self-reflection, learn from experiences and feedback, and continuously evolve and adapt your leadership style. This chapter explores the significance of self-reflection in leadership growth, the value of learning from experiences and feedback, and the process of evolving and adapting as a leader.

Section 1: The Importance of Self-Reflection in Leadership Growth
1.1 Understanding Self-Reflection:
Self-reflection is the practice of introspection and examination of one's thoughts, actions, and behaviors. It allows leaders to gain a deeper understanding of themselves and their impact on others.

1.2 Developing Self-Awareness:
Self-reflection promotes self-awareness, enabling leaders to identify their strengths, weaknesses, values, and beliefs. This awareness is crucial for effective decision-making and understanding how to leverage strengths and mitigate weaknesses.

1.3 Identifying Areas for Improvement:
Through self-reflection, leaders can recognize areas where they can improve their leadership skills, such as communication, delegation, or emotional intelligence. It

helps in setting development goals and focusing efforts on personal growth.

1.4 Cultivating Empathy and Perspective:
Self-reflection encourages leaders to consider different perspectives and empathize with others. By understanding the thoughts and feelings of team members, leaders can foster an inclusive and supportive work environment.

Section 2: Learning from Experiences and Feedback
2.1 Embracing a Growth Mindset:
Leaders should adopt a growth mindset, viewing failures and setbacks as opportunities for learning and growth. Every experience, whether positive or negative, offers valuable lessons that can shape leadership effectiveness.

2.2 Extracting Lessons Learned:
Leaders must reflect on past experiences, identifying what worked well and what could have been done differently. This retrospective analysis helps leaders gain insights into their decision-making and problem-solving abilities.

2.3 Seeking and Embracing Feedback:
Feedback from peers, superiors, and team members is a powerful tool for leadership development. Leaders should actively solicit feedback and create a safe environment where people feel comfortable providing honest input.

2.4 Incorporating Feedback into Leadership Practices:
Effective leaders integrate feedback into their ongoing development. They use feedback to refine their leadership

approach, address blind spots, and enhance their interactions with others.

Section 3: Continuously Evolving and Adapting Your Leadership Style

3.1 Embracing Change:
In today's dynamic world, leaders must be adaptable and open to change. They should embrace new ideas, technologies, and market trends, and be willing to adapt their leadership style to suit evolving circumstances.

3.2 Flexibility in Leadership Style:
Different situations may call for different leadership styles. Leaders should develop a range of leadership approaches, such as directive, participative, or transformational, and choose the most appropriate style based on the needs of the team and the situation at hand.

3.3 Emphasizing Lifelong Learning:
Leadership development is a lifelong journey. Engaging in continuous learning through reading, attending seminars, workshops, or seeking mentorship ensures leaders stay updated, acquire new skills, and remain relevant in a changing environment.

3.4 Encouraging Experimentation and Innovation:
Leaders should create a culture that values experimentation and innovation. By encouraging team members to think creatively and take calculated risks, leaders foster a climate of growth and continuous improvement.

Conclusion:
Reflecting and evolving as a leader is a dynamic process that requires self-awareness, a growth mindset, and a commitment to learning and development. By embracing self-reflection, learning from experiences and feedback, and adapting their leadership style, leaders can enhance their effectiveness, build strong relationships, and drive positive change within their organizations.

Chapter 26: Leading with Empathy and Compassion

Introduction:
In today's fast-paced and competitive world, the role of empathy and compassion in leadership cannot be overstated. Leaders who genuinely understand and care for their team members can foster an environment of trust, collaboration, and growth. This chapter explores the significance of empathy and compassion in leadership, discusses how to create a supportive and caring environment, and introduces the concept of servant leadership.

1. The Role of Empathy and Compassion in Leadership:
Empathy and compassion are essential qualities for effective leaders. When leaders empathize with their team members, they can understand their perspectives, challenges, and emotions. This understanding helps leaders make informed decisions and provide support in a way that resonates with their team. Compassion, on the other hand, involves a genuine concern for the well-being and development of others. It goes beyond sympathy and involves taking action to alleviate suffering or promote growth.

2. Creating a Supportive and Caring Environment:
Leaders can foster a supportive and caring environment by prioritizing the well-being of their team members. Here are some strategies to create such an environment:

a. Active Listening: Leaders should actively listen to their team members' concerns, ideas, and feedback without judgment. This shows that their perspectives are valued and encourages open communication.

b. Emotional Intelligence: Leaders with high emotional intelligence can understand and manage their own emotions while empathizing with others. This skill allows them to respond appropriately to their team members' needs and create a positive work environment.

c. Recognizing Achievements: Acknowledging and celebrating the achievements of team members fosters a sense of accomplishment and motivates them to perform at their best. This recognition can be public or private, depending on the individual's preference.

d. Flexibility and Work-Life Balance: Supporting work-life balance initiatives and offering flexibility, when possible, can show team members that their personal lives are valued. This helps reduce stress and burnout, leading to increased productivity and job satisfaction.

e. Development and Growth Opportunities: Providing opportunities for learning and growth demonstrates a leader's investment in their team members' long-term success. This can include training programs, mentorship, or challenging assignments that allow individuals to expand their skills and knowledge.

3. Practicing Servant Leadership:

Servant leadership is a leadership philosophy that emphasizes serving others first. A servant leader focuses on the well-being and growth of their team members, placing their needs above their own. Here are some key principles of servant leadership:

a. Empowerment: Servant leaders empower their team members by providing them with the necessary tools, resources, and authority to excel in their roles. They trust their team members and encourage autonomy.

b. Collaboration: Servant leaders foster a collaborative and inclusive culture where everyone's opinions and contributions are valued. They actively seek input from their team members and involve them in decision-making processes.

c. Service: Servant leaders prioritize the needs of their team members, ensuring they have the support and guidance required to succeed. They remove obstacles and act as advocates for their team, helping them overcome challenges.

d. Growth and Development: Servant leaders are committed to the growth and development of their team members. They provide opportunities for learning, mentorship, and skill-building, enabling individuals to reach their full potential.

e. Ethical Behavior: Servant leaders lead by example and uphold high ethical standards. They demonstrate integrity, honesty, and transparency in their actions, earning the trust and respect of their team.

Conclusion:
Leaders who lead with empathy and compassion create environments where individuals feel valued, supported, and motivated to perform at their best. By practicing servant leadership and fostering a caring culture, leaders can build strong, cohesive teams that achieve remarkable results while prioritizing the well-being and growth of their members. Embracing these principles of leadership not only benefits the individuals involved but also contributes to a more compassionate and empathetic society as a whole.

Chapter 27: Overcoming Leadership Challenges

Introduction:
In the dynamic and complex world of leadership, challenges are inevitable. Effective leaders are those who can navigate through obstacles and overcome them with resilience and perseverance. This chapter will explore common challenges faced by leaders, strategies for overcoming these obstacles, and the importance of developing resilience and perseverance.

1. Common Challenges Faced by Leaders:
a. Resistance to Change: Leaders often face resistance from team members or stakeholders when implementing new strategies or making organizational changes. Overcoming resistance requires effective communication, involvement of key stakeholders, and addressing concerns through open dialogue.

b. Decision-Making: Leaders are constantly faced with making tough decisions, which can be challenging due to uncertainty, time constraints, or conflicting interests. Developing decision-making skills, seeking input from diverse perspectives, and gathering relevant information can help leaders make informed choices.

c. Managing Conflict: Conflict is a natural part of any organization, and leaders must address it effectively to maintain a productive work environment. This involves promoting open communication, active listening, and facilitating conflict resolution processes when necessary.

d. Building and Motivating a Team: Leaders face challenges in building a cohesive and high-performing team. Overcoming this challenge requires effective communication, setting clear expectations, providing constructive feedback, fostering a positive work culture, and recognizing and rewarding achievements.

e. Adapting to Change: Leaders must be adaptable in the face of rapidly changing environments, technologies, and market conditions. They need to embrace continuous learning, encourage innovation, and promote a growth mindset within the organization.

2. Strategies for Overcoming Obstacles:
a. Communication: Effective communication is essential for overcoming various challenges. Leaders should clearly articulate their vision, actively listen to their team members, provide regular updates, and encourage open and transparent communication throughout the organization.

b. Collaboration and Empowerment: Encouraging collaboration and empowering team members fosters a sense of ownership and engagement. Leaders should involve their team in decision-making, delegate responsibilities, and create an environment where diverse perspectives are valued.

c. Emotional Intelligence: Developing emotional intelligence enables leaders to understand and manage their own emotions and those of others. This skill helps leaders navigate conflicts, build relationships, and inspire trust and motivation within their teams.

d. Continuous Learning: Leaders should embrace a mindset of continuous learning to stay ahead of challenges. This involves seeking feedback, staying updated on industry trends, attending relevant workshops or seminars, and investing in personal and professional development.

3. Developing Resilience and Perseverance:
a. Self-Reflection: Leaders should engage in regular self-reflection to identify their strengths, weaknesses, and areas for growth. This self-awareness helps them build resilience by recognizing their own limitations and developing strategies to overcome obstacles.

b. Building Support Networks: Leaders should surround themselves with a strong support network, including mentors, peers, and advisors. These individuals can provide guidance, advice, and emotional support during challenging times.

c. Maintaining a Positive Mindset: Cultivating a positive mindset helps leaders navigate setbacks and challenges. They should focus on the lessons learned from failures, celebrate small wins, and maintain optimism in the face of adversity.

d. Perseverance: Leaders must be resilient and persevere in the face of challenges. This involves staying committed to their goals, being persistent in finding solutions, and viewing setbacks as opportunities for growth and improvement.

Conclusion:
Leadership challenges are inevitable, but with the right strategies and mindset, leaders can overcome them. By developing effective communication skills, fostering collaboration and empowerment, and cultivating resilience and perseverance, leaders can navigate obstacles and emerge stronger. Remember, leadership is a journey of continuous growth, and each challenge presents an opportunity to learn and improve.

Chapter 28: Leaving a Leadership Legacy

Crafting a Meaningful Leadership Legacy:
As a leader, one of the most important aspects of your role is to leave a lasting impact on your organization and the people you lead. Crafting a meaningful leadership legacy involves defining your values, purpose, and vision for your organization. It requires intentional actions and decisions that align with your core principles and contribute to the long-term success and growth of your team.

To craft a meaningful leadership legacy, start by reflecting on your personal values and how they relate to your leadership style. Identify the principles and beliefs that guide your decision-making process and shape your interactions with others. Consider the type of culture you want to foster within your organization and how you can create an environment that encourages collaboration, innovation, and personal growth.

Succession Planning and Developing Future Leaders:
A critical aspect of leaving a leadership legacy is succession planning. Succession planning involves identifying and developing future leaders who can carry on your vision and values after you have moved on from your role. It ensures continuity and minimizes disruptions during leadership transitions.

Begin by identifying potential successors within your organization who demonstrate the necessary skills, qualities, and potential to take on leadership roles. Provide them with opportunities for growth and development, such as mentoring, coaching, and training programs. Encourage them to take on challenging assignments and gradually increase their responsibilities to prepare them for future leadership positions.

Additionally, it's essential to create a culture of leadership development throughout your organization. Encourage all employees to develop their leadership skills, regardless of their current roles. Offer leadership training programs, workshops, and resources that empower individuals to enhance their capabilities and take on leadership responsibilities when the time comes.

Creating a Lasting Impact in Your Organization and Beyond: Leaving a leadership legacy extends beyond your immediate organization. It involves creating a lasting impact that transcends boundaries and positively influences the broader community or industry.

Consider how you can contribute to the greater good by leveraging your position and resources. This may involve initiating corporate social responsibility programs, supporting philanthropic endeavors, or engaging in sustainable business practices. By aligning your organization's goals with social and environmental causes, you can leave a legacy that goes beyond financial success.

Furthermore, share your knowledge and experiences with others through speaking engagements, writing articles or books, or mentoring aspiring leaders. By sharing your wisdom and insights, you can inspire and guide future generations of leaders, leaving a lasting impact that extends far beyond your time in a leadership role.

In summary, leaving a leadership legacy involves crafting a meaningful impact through intentional actions and decisions. It requires succession planning and developing future leaders who can carry on your vision and values. Lastly, it encompasses creating a lasting impact in your organization and beyond by contributing to the greater good and sharing your knowledge and experiences with others. By focusing on these aspects, you can leave a legacy that positively influences your organization, the people you lead, and society as a whole.

Chapter 29: Leading with Purpose and Passion

Introduction:
In this chapter, we will explore the importance of purpose-driven leadership and how it can inspire and motivate both leaders and their teams. We will delve into the significance of discovering and pursuing passions, as well as how leaders can inspire others to find purpose in their work. By embracing purpose and passion, leaders can create a positive and fulfilling work environment that fosters growth and success.

1. The Power of Purpose-Driven Leadership:
Purpose-driven leadership involves aligning your leadership style and actions with a larger mission or purpose that goes beyond personal gain. When leaders lead with purpose, they tap into a powerful source of inspiration and motivation that fuels their decision-making and influences their interactions with others. Purpose-driven leaders understand that their role extends beyond mere task delegation; they strive to make a meaningful impact and contribute to something greater.

2. Discovering and Pursuing Your Passions:
Passions are the driving forces behind our deepest motivations and desires. As a leader, it is essential to discover and understand your passions. Reflect on the activities that bring you joy, the causes that ignite your enthusiasm, and the skills you love to utilize. By identifying your passions, you can align your work and leadership style with what truly matters to you. This alignment creates a

sense of authenticity and fulfillment, enabling you to lead with greater purpose and passion.

3. Inspiring Others to Find Purpose in Their Work:
Leaders have the ability to inspire and empower their team members to find purpose in their work. Here are some strategies to help you achieve this:

a. Communicate the larger purpose: Clearly articulate the organization's mission and how each individual's work contributes to it. Help your team members understand the impact they are making and how their efforts align with the greater purpose.

b. Connect personal passions: Encourage your team members to explore and identify their own passions. Seek opportunities to align their roles and responsibilities with their passions, whenever possible. When people can connect their personal interests with their work, they are more likely to find meaning and purpose in what they do.

c. Provide growth and development opportunities: Help your team members grow both personally and professionally. Offer training, mentorship, and challenging assignments that allow individuals to develop new skills and pursue their passions. When people feel supported and encouraged to pursue their interests, they are more likely to find purpose in their work.

d. Recognize and celebrate achievements: Acknowledge and appreciate the contributions of your team members.

Celebrate milestones and achievements, both big and small. This recognition reinforces the sense of purpose and motivates individuals to continue striving for excellence.

Conclusion:
Leading with purpose and passion is a transformative approach to leadership. By understanding your own purpose, pursuing your passions, and inspiring others to find purpose in their work, you can create a work environment that fosters personal growth, engagement, and success. When leaders lead with purpose, they become catalysts for positive change and inspire others to unlock their full potential. Embrace purpose-driven leadership and watch as your team thrives and achieves remarkable results.

Chapter 30: The Journey Continues

Reflections on the leadership journey:

As I look back on the leadership journey we have embarked upon together, I am filled with a sense of gratitude and awe. We have faced numerous challenges, celebrated victories, and learned invaluable lessons along the way. The path of leadership is never smooth, but it is in those moments of adversity that our true strength and resilience are revealed.

Throughout this journey, I have come to understand that leadership is not merely about holding a position of authority or power. True leadership lies in the ability to inspire, guide, and empower others to reach their full potential. It is about fostering an environment of trust, collaboration, and innovation. It is about leading by example and embodying the values and principles we hold dear.

I have learned that leadership is a continuous process of self-reflection and growth. It requires us to constantly challenge our assumptions, expand our knowledge, and develop new skills. It is through this ongoing commitment to personal and professional development that we can truly make a lasting impact.

Encouragement for ongoing growth and development:

As our journey continues, I encourage you to embrace a mindset of lifelong learning and growth. Seek out opportunities to broaden your horizons, whether through formal education, mentorship, or self-study. Surround yourself with individuals who inspire and challenge you and be open to their perspectives and insights. Remember that leadership is not a solitary endeavor; it thrives in a community of like-minded individuals who support and uplift one another.

Take risks and step outside of your comfort zone. Growth occurs when we push ourselves beyond what we believe to be possible. Embrace failure as a stepping stone to success and learn from every setback. Remember that setbacks are not indicative of your worth or abilities; they are simply part of the journey.

Celebrate your successes, no matter how small. Recognize the progress you have made and use it as fuel to propel you forward. Acknowledge the efforts of your team and foster a culture of appreciation and gratitude. Together, we can create an environment where everyone feels valued and motivated to give their best.

Final thoughts and call to action:

As we conclude this chapter and venture into the next phase of our journey, I want to leave you with a final thought and a call to action. Leadership is not a destination; it is a continuous, ever-evolving process. It is not about reaching a specific goal or achieving a certain level of status. It is about making a positive difference in the lives of others and leaving a lasting legacy.

So, I urge you to commit yourself wholeheartedly to the pursuit of meaningful leadership. Embrace the challenges that lie ahead with courage and determination. Remember that your actions have the power to shape the world around you. Be a force for positive change and inspire those around you to do the same.

Together, let us continue this journey of leadership, bound by a shared vision and a relentless pursuit of excellence. The world needs leaders who are compassionate, courageous, and visionary. Will you answer the call? Will you step up and make a difference?

The choice is yours. The journey continues.

In conclusion, "Rise to Lead: Unleashing Your Potential" is a transformative journey that empowers individuals to unlock their true leadership potential. Throughout this guide, we have explored key principles and strategies that can help individuals develop their leadership skills and take charge of their professional and personal lives. Here are some final thoughts and takeaways:

1. Embrace self-awareness: Self-awareness is the foundation of effective leadership. Understanding your strengths, weaknesses, values, and goals enables you to make better decisions and lead authentically.

2. Develop a growth mindset: Embrace a mindset of continuous learning and growth. Emphasize the power of resilience, adaptability, and the willingness to step outside your comfort zone.

3. Cultivate emotional intelligence: Emotional intelligence is crucial for effective leadership. Nurture your ability to understand and manage emotions, build relationships, and inspire others.

4. Communicate with impact: Strong communication skills are essential for successful leadership. Master the art of active listening, effective verbal and nonverbal communication, and the ability to convey your message clearly and persuasively.

5. Build a diverse and inclusive team: Recognize the value of diversity and inclusion in your team. Foster an environment where everyone feels heard, valued, and empowered to contribute their unique perspectives.

6. Lead with integrity and authenticity: Authentic leadership is based on honesty, transparency, and ethical decision-making. Lead by example, uphold your values, and build trust with your team and stakeholders.

7. Foster a culture of innovation and collaboration: Encourage creativity, experimentation, and collaboration within your team. Create an environment where new ideas are welcomed, and individuals are empowered to contribute their innovative solutions.

8. Embrace change and uncertainty: The ability to navigate change and uncertainty is a hallmark of effective leadership. Embrace ambiguity, adapt quickly to new circumstances, and inspire confidence in your team during times of transition.

9. Invest in your personal growth: Continuous personal growth and development are vital for long-term leadership success. Seek out opportunities for learning, whether through formal education, mentorship, networking, or self-reflection.

10. Lead with purpose: Connect with your purpose and align it with your leadership journey. Leading with purpose

gives your actions meaning and provides a sense of direction and fulfillment.

Remember, leadership is not reserved for a select few. With dedication, self-reflection, and a commitment to growth, anyone can rise to lead and unleash their potential. So, go forth with confidence, embrace challenges, and inspire others as you embark on your leadership journey.

www.ingramcontent.com/pod-product-compliance
Lightning Source LLC
Chambersburg PA
CBHW031433210526
45464CB00005B/2187